PLEASURES OF RICE COOKING

PLEASURES OF RICE COOKING

By :
Sneha R. Vij

Crest Publishing House
(A JAICO ENTERPRISE)
G-2, 16 Ansari Road, Darya Ganj
New Delhi-110 002

PLEASURES OF RICE COOKING
ISBN 81-242-0195-1

First Edition : 2000
Reprinted : 2001

Published by:
CREST PUBLISHING HOUSE
(A Jaico Enterprise)
G-2, 16 Ansari Road, Darya Ganj,
New Delhi-110 002

Printed by:
Taj Press
New Delhi-110064

INTRODUCTION

Cooking rice dishes like pulaos biryanis, khichrees etc is a subject every housewife is interested in. Besides, who does not relish rice? Rice cooking is neither difficult nor boring, if done systematically. There are people having the wrong notion that culinary art cannot be acquired through books. As a matter of fact, many housewives owe their expertise in cooking to good cookery books. Books written in simple easy-to-understand language & with detailed instructions, are indeed a boon to every housewife, especially to the newly-weds.

This book titled 'PLEASURES OF RICE COOKING' is a comprehensive yet concise guide to rice cooking, covering both, vegetarian & non-vegetarian dishes. It is intended to be of use on all occasions. It is written in a simple language & all the recipes included in it, have been tried & tested several times. The recipes are not only mouth-watering but exceptionally easy-to-prepare as well.

I take this opportunity to thank my dear mother, MRS. NANDA S. KARKHANIS who helped me in trying out all the recipes, included in this book & also encouraged me in getting this book published.

CONTENTS

PART- I

PART- II

RECIPE SECTION

PART I

A. SPECIAL MASALAS

1. PULAO MASALA

(Makes approx 4 tbsp)

Ingredients :

Small Cardamoms (peeled)	— 1 tbsp
Cinnamon	— ¾ tbsp
Cloves	— ¾ tbsp
Cumin seeds	— 1 tbsp
Mace	— 1 tbsp

Method :

1. Combine all the above ings & grind to a fine powder.
2. Store in a dry, clean jar & use as needed.

2. CURRY POWDER

(Makes approx 50 gms)

Ingredients :

Corriander seeds (roasted)	— ½ cup
Cumin seeds (roasted)	— 1/8 cup
Fenugreek seeds (roasted)	— ½ tbsp
Poppy seeds (roasted)	— 1/8 cup
Dried red chillies	— 15-20
Turmeric (chopped)	— 1"
Peppercorns	— ½ tbsp
Mustard seeds (roasted)	— ½ tbsp

Method :

1. Mix together all the above ings & grind to a fine powder.
2. Store in a clean, dry glass jar & use a needed.

3. GARAM MASALA POWDER

(Makes approx. 2 tbsps)

Ingredients :

Corriander seeds (roasted)	— 1 tbsp
Cumin seeds (roasted)	— ½ tbsp
Peppercorns (roasted)	— ½ tsp
Cardamoms (peeled & roasted)	— ½ tsp
Cinnamon (broken into bits & roasted)	— 1"
Cloves (roasted)	— 2
Nutmeg (roasted)	— 1/8
Shahjeera (roasted)	— ¼ tsp

Method :

1. Roast each of the above ings separately & grind to a fine powder.
2. Store in an airtight clean & dry jar.
3. Use as needed.

B. RICE COOKING—USEFUL TIPS

1. For cooking 1 measure of rice, the exact quantity of water of be used is 2 measures (i.e. for 1 cup rice you require 2 cups of water).

2. For garnishing pulaos, biryanis etc, fry onions with a pinch of sugar. They will turn brown faster, saving you time.

3. Add some bay leaves to raw rice when storing it. Besides keeping worms at bay, they also spread a delicious fragrance every time you open the container.

4. Add one cup of grated carrot when you cook rice. Your rice will be healthier, tastier & colourful.

C. ABBREVIATIONS COMMONLY USED

tsp	—	teaspoon /s
dtsp	—	dessertspoon /s
tbsp	—	tablespoon /s
ml	—	millilitre /s
lit	—	litre /s
fl	—	fluid
oz	—	ounce /s
lb	—	pound /s
gm	—	gram /s
kg	—	kilogram /s
^{0}C	—	degrees centigrade
^{0}F	—	degrees fahrenheit
fridge	—	refrigerator
&	—	and
"	—	inch (for e.g. 1" = 1 inch
mt	—	minute /s
hr	—	hour/s
ing	—	ingredient /s
to taste	—	as per requirement
approx	—	approximately

PART II :
RECIPE SECTION

A. RECIPES FOR RICE

1. PLAIN BOILED RICE

(Serves 2-3)

Ingredients :

Rice (washed)	— 1 cup
Water	— 2 cups
Salt	— to taste

Method :

1. Mix together all the ings & cook until the rice is tender, covered.

NOTE : *Incase you are cooking the rice in a pressure cooker, cook it upto 2 whistles.*

2. JEERA RICE

(Serves 2-3)

Ingredients :

Rice (washed)	—	1 cup
Water	—	2 cups
Cumin seeds	—	½ tsp
Ghee	—	1 tbsp
Salt	—	to taste

Method :

1. Heat the ghee in a pan, add the cumin seeds & when they crackle add the washed rice along with water & cook covered till done.

3. MASALA RICE

(Serves — 6-8)

Ingredients :

Rice (cooked with grains separate & cooled)	— 1½ cups
Gherkins (vertically slit in 4 with stalk intact)	— 6 (small)
Brinjals (vertically slit in 4 with stalk intact)	— 5 (small)
Potatoes (vertically slit in 4 with stalk intact)	— 5
Onions (vertically slit in 4 with stalk intact)	— 5
Green peas (shelled & boiled)	— 1 cup
Oil	— 5 tbsps
Salt	— to taste

To be ground to a fine paste :

Coconut (grated)	— ½
Corriander leaves (chopped)	— 1 cup
Chilli powder	— 2 tsps
Garam masala powder	— 1 tsp
Corriander-cumin powder	— 4 tsps
Asafoetida powder	— pinchful
Sugar	— 1 tsp
Salt	— to taste

Method :

1. Stuff the slit vegetables with the ground masala paste. Reserve the leftover paste.
2. Heat the oil in a pan, add the stuffed vegetables along with salt & very little water & either pressure cook or cook covered untll soft.
3. Mix the cooked rice, remaining masala paste, green peas, salt, cooked vegetables & mix well.
4. Serve hot.

4. LIME RICE

(Serves 4-5)

Ingredients :

Freshly cooked rice	— 250 gms
Lemon juice	— 1–1½ tbsp
Corriander leaves(chopped)	— ½ bunch
Green chillies (chopped)	— 3-4
Groundnuts (roasted)	— 25 gms
Urad dal	— ½ tbsp
Coconut (grated)	— ¼
Oil	— 2 tbsp
Salt	— to taste

Method :

1. Heat the oil in a pan, add the chillies, dal & grated coconut.
2. Stir on a low flame till the dal & coconut turn light brown in colour.
3. Add the groundnuts, corriander leaves, rice, salt & mix very well.
4. Remove from flame, add the lemon juice, mix well & serve.

5. GHEE RICE

(Serves 4-5)

Ingredients :

Long grained rice	— 250 gms
Ghee	— 100 gms
Raisins (fried in little ghee)	— 25 gms
Cloves	— 5-6
Onion (chopped)	— 1 (medium)
Cashewnuts (fried in little ghee)	— 25 gms
Cinnamon	— 1"
Salt	— to taste

Method :

1. Heat the ghee in a heavy-bottomed pan.
2. Add the onion, cinnamon, cloves & fry until the onions turn light brown in colour.
3. Add water (2 measures water for 1 measure rice), salt & bring to a boil.
4. Then add the rice & cook it done.
5. Add the raisins & cashewnuts, stir well & serve hot with mutton, chicken, egg or vegetable curries.

6. CURD RICE

(Serves 3-4)

Ingredients :

Rice (boiled with grains separate)	— 3 cups
Unsalted butter	— 1 tbsp
Curds (beaten)	— 3 cups
Ginger (minced)	— 1 tsp
Green chillies (minced)	— 2 tsps
Mustard seeds	— 1 tsp
Ghee or oil	— 1 tbsp
Salt	— to taste

Method :

1. Before the rice cools, add to it the unsalted butter & mix well cool.
2. Add to it all other ings (except mustard seeds & oil) & mix very well.
3. Heat the oil in a small pan & fry the mustard seeds in it till they crackle.
4. Pour this seasoning over the rice mixture & stir well.
5. Serve at once.

7. TAMARIND RICE

(Serves 3-4)

Ingredients :

Rice (boiled with grains separate)	—	3 cups
Tamarind pulp	—	½ cup
Oil	—	¼ cup
Chana dal	—	3 tbsp
Turmeric powder	—	½ tsp
Chilli powder	—	½ tsp or more
Asafoetida powder	—	$^1/_8$ tsp
Salt	—	to taste

Method :

1. Heat half the quantity of oil in a pan & fry the asafoetida & dal till the dal turns red in colour.
2. Add the tamarind pulp, chilli powder, turmeric & salt & bring the mixture to a boil.
3. Add rice & stir well remove from flame.
4. Heat the remaining oil & add to the rice.
5. Mix very well & serve warm.

8. MANGO RICE

(Serves 4-6)

Ingredients:

Rice (washed & boiled with grains separate)	— 500 gms
Groundnuts	— 100 gms
Urad dal	— 1 tsp
Chana dal	— 1 tsp
Curry leaves	— few
Oil	— 2 tbsps
Salt	— to taste

To be ground to a fine paste :

Coconut (grated)	— ½
Mustard seeds	— ½ tsp
Raw mangoes (peeled & chopped finely)	— 2
Turmeric powder	— pinchful

Method :

1. Heat the oil in a heavy-bottomed pan.
2. Add the dals, groundnuts & curry leaves & fry gently.
3. Add the mango mixture & remove from flame.
4. Add the cooked rice & mix well.
5. Your delicious mango rice is ready to be savoured & served.

9. TURMERIC RICE

(Serves 8)

Ingredients :

Long grain rice (washed & soaked in water for 30 mts)	— $2\,^2/_3$ cups
Turmeric powder	— 1 tsp
Chilli powder	— pinchful
Bay leaf	— 1
Water	— 5 cups
Salt	— to taste

Method :

1. Cook the rice in boiling salted wear with the spices & bay leaf added, until just tender, about 15 mts.
2. Dry the rice, uncovered in a moderate oven, 325^0 F, Gas Mark 3 until the grains are separate & fluffy.

10. PULAO RICE

(Serves 4)

Ingredients :

Long–grain rice (washed & soaked in water for 1 hour)	— 1 $^1/_3$ cups
Onion	— 1
Butter or ghee	— $^1/_3$ cup
Bay leaves	— 4
Turmeric powder	— ½ tsp
Water	— 2½ cups
Cloves	— 5–6
Cinnamon	— 1"
Cardamoms	— 4
Salt	— to taste

Method :

1. Fry the onion in butter or ghee till it is golden brown, then add the spices & bay leaves & fry for 2 mts.
2. Stir in the drained rice & fry for a further 2 mts.
3. Add the water & salt & bring to the boil.
4. Simmer covered over low heat until the rice is tender about 15 mts.
5. Dry the rice, uncovered in a moderate oven, 325°F, Gas Mark 3 until the grains are separate & fluffy.

11. BROWN RICE

(Serves 4-6)

Ingredients :

Rice	— 500 gms
Onions	— 2
Bay leaves	— 4
Cardamoms	— 4
Cloves	— 4
Cinnamon (broken into bits)	— 2"
Peppercorns	— 6–8
Cumin seeds	— 1 tsp
Oil	— 6–8 tbsps
Salt	— to taste

Method :

1. Fry the onions till they turn light brown in colour.
2. Add all the spices & continue frying till the onions turn dark brown.
3. Add the rice along with salt & stir fry for a minute.
4. Pour in enough water for the rice to cook.
5. Serve hot with any vegetable or meat dish.

12. OVEN-BAKED RICE

(Serves 4)

Ingredients :

Long-grain rice (washed & drained)	—	100 gms
Butter	—	25 gms
Mixed vegetables (chopped & parboiled)	—	50 gms
Water or stock	—	600 ml
Oil	—	2 tbsp
Seasoning of your choice	—	to taste

Method :

Turn the oven onto 200°C/400°F/ gas mark 7. Heat on oven-proof dish in it. In a pan melt the oil & butter together & cook the rice for 3-4 mts in the water. Add the parboiled vegetables & seasoning. Transfer the contents into the oven-proof dish, cover with buttered greaseproof paper & replace the dish in the oven. Cook for about 15-20 mts. Serve piping hot with raita of your choice.

13. COCONUT RICE (TYPE 1)

(Serves 3-4)

Ingredients :

Rice (washed & soaked in water)	— 1 cup
Coconut (grated)	— 1
Cumin seeds	— 1 tsp
Oil	— 3 tbsps
Salt	— to taste

Method :

1. Heat oil in a pan & fry the cumin seeds.
2. Add rice & fry till the rice begins to stick to the pan.
3. Add coconut milk & salt & cook on a low flame till tender.
4. Serve after cooling.

14. COCONUT RICE (TYPE 2)

(Serves 3-4)

Ingredients :

Rice (boiled with grains separate)	— 1 cup
Coconut (grated finely)	— ½ cup
Urad dal	— 1 tsp
Chana dal	— ½ tbsp
Curry leaves	— few
Green chillies (minced)	— 2
Red chillies (broken into 2 pieces each)	— 2
Mustard seeds	— ¼ tsp
Asafoetida powder	— pinchful
Cashewnuts (fried)	— 1 tbsp
Salt	— to taste
Oil	— 2 tbsps

Method :

1. Heat the oil in a pan, put in mustard seeds, dals, red chillies & asafoetida powder.
2. When the dals turn red, put in coconut, green chillies, curry leaves & fry till the coconut turns red.
3. Add rice & mix thoroughly with the coconut mixture.
4. Serve immediately garnished with cashewnuts.

15. TOMATO RICE

(Serves 3-4)

Ingredients :

Tomatoes (pureed)	—	250 gms
Rice (washed)	—	1 cup
Onion (chopped)	—	1
Green chilli (slit)	—	1
Cinnamon	—	1"
Cloves	—	2-3
Cardamoms	—	2
Mustard seeds	—	½ tsp
Cumin seeds	—	½ tsp
Oil	—	4 tbsps
Salt	—	to taste

Method :

1. Heat the oil in a heavy-bottomed large pan & fry the onions till light brown.
2. Add the full garam masala & mustard & fry for a mt.
3. Add green chilli & cumin seeds.
4. Then add the tomato puree, rice & salt to taste, along with the required quantity of water.
5. Bring to a boil & cook till the rice is done, on a low flame. Serve hot.

16. SESAME RICE

(Serves 3-4)

Ingredients :

Rice (boiled with grains separate)	— 250 gms
Sesame seeds	— 2 tbsps
Red chillies (broken into bits)	— 4-5
Lemon juice	— 1 tbsp
Curry leaves	— few
Peppercorns	— 6-8
Urad dal	— 1 tsp
Asafoetida powder	— pinchful
Salt	— to taste
Ghee	— as per need
Cashewnuts (fried)	— 1½ tbsps

Method :

1. Fry the sesame seeds, peppercorns, urad dal & asafoetida powder in a little ghee & grind to a powder.
2. Heat 1-2 tbsps ghee in a pan, add the curry leaves, the rice, powdered ings & salt along with lemon juice.
3. Mix very well & serve hot garnished with cashewnuts.

17. VEGETABLE FRIED RICE

(Serves 3-5)

Ingredients :

Rice	— 250 gms
Onions (chopped finely)	— 2
Mixed vegetables of your choice (chopped)	— 1 cup
Green chillies (chopped finely)	— 2-3
Corriander seeds	— ¼ tsp
Cloves	— 2
Peppercorns	— ¼ tsp
Oil	— 2 tsps
Salt	— to taste

Method :

1. Heat the oil in a pan & make a seasoning with green chillies, peppercorns, corriander seeds & cloves.
2. Add onions & fry till the onions turn soft & transparent.
3. Add chopped vegetables & fry lightly.
4. Add rice & fry for a while.
5. Add salt & enough water & cook till the rice is done. Serve hot.

18. CHINESE FRIED RICE

(Serves 4-5)

Ingredients :

Rice (boiled with grains separate)	—	1 cup
Spring onions (sliced thinly)	—	10
Cabbage (shredded & parboiled)	—	¼ cup
Green peas (shelled & boiled)	—	¼ cup
Ajinomoto	—	pinchful
Soya sauce	—	to taste
Salad oil	—	3 tbsps
Salt	—	to taste
Chilli sauce	—	to serve

Method :

1. Heat the oil in a heavy-bottomed pan & fry the onion in it for 2-3 mts lightly.
2. Add all ings (except the rice) & stir for sometime.
3. Add the rice & mix carefully till the rice turns light brown in colour.
4. Serve hot with chilli sauce.

19. EGG FRIED RICE

(Serves 3-4)

Ingredients :

Long grain rice (boiled)	— 1 cup
Spring onions with leaves	— 8
Eggs (beaten)	— 2
Oil	— 3 tbsps
Ajinomoto	— pinchful
Soya sauce	— to taste
Salt	— to taste
Chilli sauce	— to serve

Method :

1. Add salt to the egg & prepare a thin omelette.
2. Cut the omelette into tiny squares & keep aside.
3. Heat the oil in a pan & fry the spring onions gently, on a low flame.
4. Add salt, ajinomoto & after stirring well, add the rice, omelete squares & soya sauce.
5. Increase the heat & stir fry till the rice is well mixed with all ings & turns light brown in colour.
6. Serve hot with chilli sauce.

20. RICH SAFFRON FRIED RICE

(Serves 6-8)

Ingredients :

Long-grain rice (washed & soaked in water for 2 hrs)	— 2 cup
Green peas (shelled)	— 1 cup
Saffron (soaked in 1 tbsp water)	— ½ tsp
Cloves	— 4-5
Cinnamon	— 1"
Cardamom (black)	— 1
Peppercorns	— ½ tsp
Ghee	— as per need
Salt	— to taste
Walnuts (shelled & chopped)	— 8
Almonds (blanched & sliced)	— 15
Raisins	— 1 tbsp
Saffron	— few strands

Method :

1. Heat a little ghee in a pan & fry the dry fruits till light brown.
2. Remove & keep aside.
3. Then fry all the whole garam masala lightly.
4. Add peas & fry for 2-3 mts.
5. Fry the rice adding a little saffron mixture.
6. Add 4 cups of water & bring to a boil.
7. Reduce the flame & cook till half done.
8. Sprinkle the remaining saffron mixture over the rice & cook covered till done.
9. Serve hot garnished with walnuts, almonds, raisins & saffron strands.

21. CABBAGE RICE

(Serves 4-5)

Ingredients :

Rice	— 1 cup
Onion (sliced)	— 1
Cabbage (shredded)	— 1 cup
Green peas	— ½ cup
Coconut (grated)	— ¼
Cinnamon	— 1"
Cardamoms	— 2
Cloves	— 1-2
Garam masala powder	— 1 tsp
Chilli powder	— ½ tsp
Turmeric powder	— ¼ tsp
Lemon juice	— ½ tbsp
Oil	— 2½ tbsps
Salt	— to taste

To be ground into a fine paste :

Green chillies	— 2-3
Ginger	— ½"
Garlic	— 3-4 cloves

Method :

1. Heat the oil in a pan & add the cloves, cinnamon, cardamoms along with the onion.
2. Add all other ings (except the lemon juice) along with enough water to cook the rice.
3. Cook covered on a low flame until the rice is cooked & tender.
4. Add the lemon juice, mix well & serve hot.

22. TOMATO 'N' EGG RICE

(Serves 6-8)

Ingredients :

Long - grain rice (washed)	— 1½ cups
Cottage cheese (crushed)	— ½ cup
Tomato sauce	— ½ cup
Eggs	— 6
Onions (chopped)	— 2 (big)
Potato	— 1 (big)
Corriander leaves (chopped)	— 1 tbsp
Green chillies (chopped)	— 2-3
Ghee	— as per need
Sugar	— to taste
Salt	— to taste
Tomatoes	— 4-5

Method :

1. Heat ghee in a pan and fry the chopped onions. Add rice, salt and enough water for the rice to boil partially.
2. Once the water evaporates, divide the rice into 2 parts and put in 2 separators of cooker. Cut the tomatoes into halves and empty the centre.
3. Make 3 hollows in the rice and place in separate or with hand and place bowl like tomatoes in them. Break one egg and place it in a tomato bowl without beating. Sprinkle cottage cheese, green chillies, corriander leaves and salt.

4. Taking the middle of 3 eggs as centre, draw deep dividing lines on the rice and fill the lines with tomato sauce. Repeat the same procedure in the other separator too.

5. Put a little water in cooker and place a grid. Fix both separators on it and close the cooker. Remove from flame as soon as pressure is reached at and cook the rice in steam till heat subsides. Take out the chunks of rice carefully and place them straight on two plates.

23. YELLOW RICE WITH CHICKEN CURRY

(Serves 4-5)

Ingredients :

For the rice :

Long grain rice (washed & soaked in water for 30 mts)	—$1\frac{1}{3}$ cups
Butter	— 2 tbsps
Turmeric powder	— 1 tsp
Cloves	— 1 tsp
Cumin seeds (roasted & powdered)	— 1 tsp
Boiling water	— $2\frac{1}{2}$ cups
Cucumber (cut into strips)	— 1
Salt	— to taste

For the Chicken Curry :

Chicken (jointed & washed)	— 1
Onion (chopped)	— 1

Garlic (minced)	— 2-3 cloves
Butter	— ¼ cup
Curry powder	— 2 tsps
Chilli powder	— 1 tsp
Tomatoes (chopped)	— 3-4
Water	— $^2/_3$ tbsps
Curds	— 2 tbsps
Salt	— to taste

Method :

1. Heat the ¼ cup ghee in a pan & fry the onion & garlic lightly. Add the curry powder, chilli powder, chicken pieces & salt.
2. Fry until the chicken pieces turn brown all over stirring often.
3. Add the water & cook covered for about 40-45 mts.
4. Drain the rice thoroughly & fry it in the butter over a medium flame, until golden & transparent.
5. Add all other ings mentioned under rice & simmer until the rice is well - cooked & dry.
6. Add the tomatoes & curds to the chicken & simmer for 5-7 mts.
7. Serve the chicken curry with the yellow rice.

24. SWEET RICE (TYPE 1)

(Serves 5-7)

Ingredients :

Long-grain rice (washed and soaked in water for 30 mts)	— 250 gm
Milk	— ½ lt
Sugar	— 200 gm
Ghee	— 6 tsps
Cloves	— 3
Cinnamon	— ½"
Cardamoms	— 3
Almonds	— 1 tbsp
Raisins	— 1 tbsp
Silver paper	— 2 sheets

Method :

1. Drain the rice thoroughly & roast in a pan until it turns light brown in colour.
2. Mix the rice & milk in vessel & cook covered over low heat till all the milk dries up.
3. Add sugar & remove from flame.
4. Heat ghee in a pan & fry the cloves, cinnamon & cardamom for 1-2 mts.
5. Add the cooked rice & fry over a low flame till the ghee separates.
6. Garnish with almonds, raisins & silver paper.

25. SWEET RICE (TYPE 2)

(Serves 5-7)

Ingredients :

Rice	— 200 gms
Moong dal (roasted till red)	— 50 gms
Milk	— ½ litre
Ghee	— 100 gms
Jaggery (grated)	— ½ cup
Cardamoms (powdered)	— ½ tsp
Cashewnuts (fried)	— 1 tbsp
Raisins (fried)	— 1 tbsp
Nutmeg (grated)	— ¼ tsp

Method :

1. Heat the ghee in a pan, add rice, dal, milk & cook till soft.
2. Add jaggery, nutmeg, cardamom & cook on a low flame till the jaggery is dissolved & absorbed into the rice.
3. Serve hot garnished with nuts & raisins.

26. SPANISH RICE

(Serves 4-6)

Ingredients :

Rice (boiled with grains separate)	— 1½ cups
French beans (chopped & boiled)	— 100 gms
Potatoes (chopped & boiled)	— 100 gms
Carrots (chopped & boiled)	— 100 gms
Green peas (shelled & boiled)	— 100 gms
Tomato (chopped)	— 1
Onion (chopped)	— 1
Capsicum (chopped)	— 1
Curds (beaten)	— 2 tbsp
Kashmiri chillies	— 10
Garlic (peeled)	— 10 cloves
Garam masala powder	— 1 tsp
Oil	— 6 tbsps
Tomato (cut into slices)	— to garnish
Cheese (grated)	— to garnish
Salt	— to taste

Method :

1. Roast the chillies without oil & pound along with the garlic.
2. Heat the oil in a heavy-bottomed large pan add the onions & fry for one mt.
3. Add the pounded chilli mixture & fry for 1-2 mts.
4. Add the tomato, capsicum, curds & cook for 3-4 mts.
5. Add the cooked vegetables, garam masala powder, salt, rice & mix well.
6. Grease a baking dish & transfer the rice into it.
7. Cover with tomato slices & grated cheese.
8. Bake in a hot oven at 400°F for about 10 mts.

27. RICE WITH CHICKEN GRAVY

(Serves 4-5)

Ingredients :

Chicken (jointed & washed thoroughly)	— 1
Rice (boiled with grains separate)	— 2 cups
Onion (chopped)	— 1
Tomatoes	— 2
Ginger	— ½"
Green chillies	— 6
Corriander leaves	— handful
Eggs (hard boiled, shelled & quartered)	— 4
Groundnuts (roasted)	— 1½ cups
Corriander-cumin powder	— 1 tsp
Garam masala powder	— 1 tsp
Turmeric powder	— ½ tsp
Chilli powder	— to taste
Curds (beaten)	— 1 cup
Salt	— to taste
Oil	— 3 tbsps

Method :

1. Grind the onions, ginger, chillies & corriander leaves to a fine paste.
2. Mix this paste with the spices, curds, tomatoes & groundnuts.
3. Heat oil in pan add the curd mixture along with the chicken & cook on a medium flame until the chicken is tender & gravy thick.
4. Put the rice in the centre of a serving plate, arrange the chicken around it & serve garnished with eggs.

28. SHAHI CHANA DAL RICE

(Serves 3-4)

Ingredients :

Long grain rice (soaked in water for 30 mts)	— 1 cup
Chana dal (soaked in water for 30 mts)	— ½ cup
Dates	— 100 gms
Asafoetida	— pinchful
Water	— 3 cups
Ghee	— 3 tbsps
Salt	— to taste

Method :

1. Heat 1 tbsp ghee in a pan, add asafoetida, dal & water & cook the chana dal partially.
2. When the dal is half cooked, add rice, salt & cook till done on a low flame.
3. Place the vessel on a hot tawa reduce flame, add the remaining ghee & dates.
4. Cook till the dates soften a little & serve hot.

29. ITALIAN STYLE RICE (TYPE 1)

(Serves 3-5)

Ingredients :

Long grain rice	— 1½ cups
Green peas	— 2 cups
Parsley (minced)	— 1 cup
Cheese (grated)	— ½ cup
Saffron (dissolved in 1 tsp warm milk)	— few strands
Pepper	— to taste
Salt	— to taste
Milk	— ½ cup

Method :

1. Put rice together with peas & parsley in a pan.
2. Put in salt & cover with 2½ cups water & ½ cup milk.
3. Bring to a boil, reduce heat & cook till the rice is tender & dry.
4. Mix in cheese & saffron mixture.
5. Serve topped with tomato or any other sauce of your choice.

30. ITALIAN STYLE RICE (TYPE 2)

(Serves 3-5)

Ingredients :

Rice	—	1½ cups
Onion (chopped finely)	—	1
French beans	—	10-12
Carrot	—	1
Tomato puree	—	8 tbsps
Cooking cheese (grated)	—	100 gms
Sugar	—	1 tsp
Salt	—	to taste
Ghee	—	2 tbsps

Method :

1. Heat ghee in a pan & fry the onions lightly.
2. Add the rice & vegetables & cook for 3 mts.
3. Add 1 cup water, puree, sugar, salt & cook for another 30 mts.
4. When the rice is almost cooked, add half the cheese & cook covered for a few mts.
5. Sprinkle the remaining cheese on top & serve hot.

31. GREEN PEA RICE

(Serves 3-4)

Ingredients :

Long grain rice	— 1 cup
Green peas (shelled)	— ½ cup
Ghee	— 2 tbsps
Water	— 2 cups
Cinnamon (broken into bits)	— ½"
Cardamom	— 1
Cloves	— 2
Salt	— to taste

To be ground to a fine paste :

Onion (chopped)	— 1
Green chillies	— 3-4
Coriander leaves	— ½ tsp
Ginger	— ½"

Method :

1. Heat the ghee in a pan, add the full garam masala along with green peas & 2 cups of water & cook on a low flame until the peas are half cooked.
2. Add the rice, ground masala paste, salt & continue cooking until done on a low flame.
3. Serve hot with kadhi.

32. KEEMA RICE

(Serves 4-5)

Ingredients :

Rice (washed)	— 200 gms
Mutton keema (washed thoroughly)	— 250 gms
Onion (chopped finely)	— 1
Tomato (chopped finely)	— 1
Green chillies (chopped finely)	— 1-2
Corriander leaves (chopped finely)	— 1 tbsp
Ginger-garlic paste	— ¼ tsp
Saffron	— few strands
Garam masala powder	— ½ tsp
Mustard seeds	— ¼ tsp
Cumin seeds	— 1 tsp
Oil	— 5 tbsps
Salt	— to taste

Method :

1. Heat the oil in large heavy-bottomed pan & fry the onion till light brown.
2. Add the ginger-garlic paste, tomato, chillies, corriander cumin seeds, mustard seeds & garam masala powder & cook on a low flame for 2-3 mts.
3. Add the keema & cook stirring often for about 5-6 mts.
4. Add the rice, saffron & sufficient water.
5. Cook covered on a low flame till the rice is done.
6. Serve hot with raita.

33. STEAMED RICE WITH SAUSAGE

(Serves 3-4)

Ingredients :

Long grain rice (washed & soaked in water for 1 hour)	— 2 cups
Sausages	— 2
Water	— 2 cups
Salt	— to taste

Method :

1. Put the sausages & salt into the rice & cover the bowl.
2. Place the rice bowl in a pan of water & cook till the rice is done.
3. Serve hot.

34. SPICY BURMESE RICE

(Serves 3-4)

Ingredients :

Long-grain rice (boiled with grains separate)	— 3 cups
Oil	— ¼ cup
Salt	— to taste

To be deep fried separately in hot oil & powdered coarsely :

Peanuts	— ½ cup
Red chillies (deseeded)	— 12
Gram (roasted)	— ½ cup
Garlic	— 10-12 cloves

Method :

1. Heat the oil in a non-stick pan, add rice, powdered ings, salt & fry very well for 5-7 mts.
2. Serve piping hot.

35. SHRIMP EGG RICE

(Serves 4-5)

Ingredients :

Long-grain rice (boiled with grains seperate)	—	50 gms
Shrimps (deveined)	—	150 gms
Green peas (shelled & boiled in salted water)	—	handful
Onions (chopped)	—	2 (big)
Garlic (shredded finely)	—	5-6 cloves
Eggs (beaten)	—	2
Oil	—	½ cup
Soya sauce	—	2 tbsps
Salt	—	to taste

Method :

1. Heat 1 tbsp oil in a non-stick pan & fry the onions lightly.
2. Add the eggs, scramble & remove from flame. Keep aside.
3. In the same pan, heat 1 tbsp of oil & fry the garlic, peas & shrimps till golden & done. Keep aside.
4. Heat the remaining oil in the same pan & fry the rice over an high flame, adding salt to taste.
5. Stir in the shrimp mixture, scrambled eggs & soya sauce. Mix thoroughly & serve piping hot.

36. CHINESE CHOW FRIED RICE

(Serves 6-8)

Ingredients :

Long-grain rice (cooked with grains separate & cooled)	— 500 gms
Chicken or mutton (cooked & shredded)	— 125 gm
Prawns (shelled, cooked & chopped)	— 125 gm
Green peas (parboiled in salted water)	— 2 tbsp
Onion (chopped)	— 1 big
Egg (beaten)	— 1
Ajinomoto	— pinchful
Oil	— ½ cup
Soya sauce	— to taste
Salt	— to taste

Method :

1. Heat 1 tbsp oil in a pan & pour in the egg.
2. Scramble & keep aside.
3. Heat the remaining oil in a big non-stick pan & fry the peas for 2-3 mts.
4. Add the chicken or mutton prawns & the onions & fry for about 5 mts.
5. Lastly, add the rice, ajinomoto, soya sauce, salt & fry for 1-2 mts.
6. Serve hot garnished with the scrambled egg.

37. MUSHROOM FRIED RICE

(Serves 4)

Ingredients :

Long-grain rice (boiled with grains separate & cooled)	— 100 gms
Spring onions (chopped finely)	— 4
Spring onion tops (chopped finely)	— 1 cup
Mushrooms (sliced)	— ½ cup
Soya sauce	— 4 tbsp
Ajinomoto	— pinchful
Oil	— 3 tbsp
Salt	— to taste

Method :

1. Heat the oil in a large non-stick pan & stir-fry the onions, mushrooms, ajinomoto & salt for about 3-4 mts over an high flame.
2. Add the rice, soya sauce, spring onion tops & stir-fry for another 4-5 mts.
3. Serve piping hot.

38. CHICKEN-WALNUT RICE

(Serves 3-4)

Ingredients :

Long-grained rice (boiled with grains separate & cooled)	— 2 cups
Chicken breast (boned & cut into very thin strips)	— 1
Walnuts (chopped coarsely & deep fried till golden)	— ½ cup
Onions (sliced thinly)	— 2 (medium)
Celery (sliced)	— 1 stick
Salad oil	— ¼ cup
Chicken stock	— 2 cups
Ajinomoto	— pinchful
Cornflour	— 2 tbsp
Vinegar	— 1 tbsp
Soya sauce	— 1-2 tsp
Sugar	— to taste
Salt	— to taste

Method :

1. Heat oil in a pan & stir-fry the chicken pieces over a high flame for 7-8 mts with little salt.
2. Remove & keep aside. To the same oil, add celery, onions & stir-fry for 2-3 mts.
3. Mix together the soya sauce, vinegar, cornflour & sugar in a small bowl with the chicken stock & pour over the onion mixture.
4. Cook till the sauce thickens. Then add to it the chicken & walnuts. Mix in the rice lastly & serve at once.

Note : *You can also serve the chicken sauce & rice separately if desired.*

39. PEANUT RICE

(Serves 2-3)

Ingredients :

Long-grain rice (boiled with grains seperate)	— 2 cups
Peanuts (roasted)	— ½ cups
Onion (chopped finely)	— 1 (big)
Coriander leaves (chopped)	— 1 tbsp
Coconut (grated)	— ½ cup
Sesame seeds	— 1 tsp
Mustard seeds	— ½ tsp
Chilli powder	— ½ tsp
Curry leaves	— few
Oil	— 2 tbsps
Turmeric powder	— ¼ tsp
Salt	— to taste

Method :

1. Heat the oil in a non-stick pan & add the mustard seeds.
2. When they crackle, add the curry leaves & powdered spices & stir for a mt.
3. Add the onion & sesame seeds & when golden, add the coconut, peanuts & fry well.
4. Add the rice, mix well, garnish with corriander leaves & serve at once.

40. MEXICAN RICE

(Serves 3-4)

Ingredients :

Long-grain rice (washed & drained)	— 2 cups
Chicken (cut into medium-size pieces)	— 1 (medium)
Garlic (ground to a paste)	— 1 tsp
Tomatoes (chopped finely)	— 2
Oil	— 4 tbsp
Chilli powder	— 1½ tbsp
Chicken stock	— 4 cups
Pepper	— to taste
Salt	— to taste

Method :

1. Heat the oil in a pan & stir-fry the chicken pieces over an high flame till well-browned. Remove & keep aside.
2. In the same oil, fry the onions, garlic, chilli powder & salt for 5 mts.
3. Add the rice, chicken, pepper & the stock.
5. Stir well & cook covered till almost cooked.
4. Then stir-in the tomatoes & cook over a low flame until the rice is completely cooked. Serve hot.

41. PUNJABI NAMKEEN CHAWAL

(Serves 3-4)

Ingredients :

Hushed Urad dal (washed & soaked in water for 4 hrs.)	—	½ cup
Rice (washed & drained)	—	1 cup
Onions (chopped finely)	—	2
Ginger-garlic paste	—	1 tsp
Chilli powder	—	½ tsp
Turmeric powder	—	¼ tsp
Gram flour	—	1 tbsp
Cloves	—	3
Cinnamon	—	1"
Bay leaves	—	2
Black cardamoms	—	2
Shahjeera	—	½ tsp
Ghee	—	as per need
Salt	—	to taste

Method :

1. Cook the soaked dal in little water till soft & tender.
2. Cool & mix well with your hands to mash it.
3. Add to it the ginger-garlic paste, powdered spices, gramflour, salt & mix well.
4. Heat ghee in a pan, prepare small balls with the dal mixture & fry till golden. Drain & keep aside.
5. Heat 2 tbsp ghee in a pan & fry the whole garam masala till brown.
6. Add the rice, fry a while & cook with 2 cups of hot water till half-done.
7. Add to it the fried balls, cover & cook over a low flame till fully cooked.

(B) RECIPES FOR PULAOS

1. VEGETABLE PULAO (TYPE 1)

(Serves 4-6)

Ingredients :

Long - grain rice (washed)	— 500 gms
Onions (sliced & fried in oil till crisp)	— 2
Potatoes (boiled, sliced & fried)	— 2
Green peas (shelled)	— 100 gms
Cauliflower (broken into flowerettes)	— 100 gms
Carrots (chopped finely)	— 100 gms
French beans (chopped finely)	— 100 gms
Green chillies (chopped finely)	— 4-5
Mint leaves (chopped finely)	— 2 tbsps
Coriander leaves (chopped finely)	— 2 tbsps

Pulao masala	—	1½ tsp
Curds	—	3 thsps
Oil	—	¼ cup + 5 tbsps
Salt	—	to taste
Saffron essence	—	¼ tsp
Eggs (hard - boiled)	—	to garishe (optional)

Method :

1. Heat ¼ cup oil in frying pan & fry the onions till golden.
2. In the same oil fry the potatoes & keep aside.
3. Then fry the french beans, carrots & cauliflower together till light brown.
4. Also fry the green peas & keep aside.
5. In a large heavy-bottomed pan, mix all the ings together with the rice.
6. Add saffron essence & 5 tbsp oil as well.
7. Add enough water for the rice to cook.
8. Serve hot garnished with sliced boiled eggs.

2. VEGETABLE PULAO (TYPE 2)

(Serves 4-6)

Ingredients :

Long grain rice	— 500 gms
Green peas (shelled)	— 250 gms
Carrots (scraped & chopped into small pieces)	— 2
French beans (chopped finely)	— 150 gms
Tomatoes (chopped)	— 2
Brinjals (chopped into small pieces)	— 2
Capsicums (cubed)	— 2
Onions (chopped)	— 2
Garlic (minced)	— 4 cloves
Green chillies (chopped)	— 6
Cloves	— 4
Cinnamon	— 1"
Chilli powder	— 1½ tsp
Turmeric powder	— ½ tsp
Coconut (grated & ground to paste)	— 1

Ghee	— 250 gms
Corriander leaves (chopped)	— 1½ tbsps
Lemon juice	— 1 tbsp
Salt	— to taste

To be roasted (without oil) & ground to a fine paste :

Peppercorns	— 12
Cloves	— 4
Cinnamon	— 1"
Poppy seeds	— 1 tbsp
Cumin seeds	— 1 tsp
Corriander seeds	— 2 tsps

To be ground to a fine paste :

Onions (chopped)	— 2
Garlic	— 4 cloves
Tamarind	— lemon-sized ball

Method :

1. Heat the ghee in a large heavy - bottomed pan & stir —fry the onions (2), green chillies, minced garlic, cloves, cinnamon for a mt.
2. Add chilli powder, turmeric, peas, carrots & french beans along with ½ cup of water & salt. Parboil these vegetables.
3. Then add brinjals, capsicums & tomatoes.
4. Also add the masala pastes, mix well & cook till almost done.
5. Then add the rice & coconut paste along with enough water to cook the rice & cook till done. Serve hot.

3. VEGETABLE PULAO (TYPE 3)

(Serves 4)

Ingredients :

Long grain rice	— 1 cup
Bean dal (sprouted)	— 1 cup
Onions (chopped)	— 2
Onions (slit into 4 with stalks intact)	— 225 gms
Potatoes (slit into 4 with stalks intact)	— 225 gms
Garlic (minced)	— 2 cloves
Coconut (grated)	— ½
Turmeric powder	— ¼ tsp
Oil	— as per need
Salt	— to taste

To be ground to a fine paste :

Coconut (grated)	— ¼
Corriander leaves (chopped)	— ½ cup
Chilli powder	— 1 tsp
Turmeric powder	— ¼ tsp
Garam masala powder	— ½ tsp

Corriander-cumin powder	—	2 tsps
Salt	—	to taste
Sugar	—	to taste

Method :

1. Fry the oil in hot oil till golden brown & crisp. Keep aside.
2. Add 2½ cups to the grated coconut & blend in a liquidiser & strain the extracted coconut milk.
3. Stuff the slits on the onions and potatoes with the ground masala paste. Keep aside the remaining masala.
4. Heat oil in pan, add the crushed garlic & fry gently. Add the rice, dal, coconut milk, salt, turmeric powder & cook covered till almost done.
5. Then add the remaining masala mixture & cook till fully cooked. Serve hot garnished with fried onions.

4. VEGETABLE CORN PULAO

(Serves 3)

Ingredients :

Long grain rice (boiled with grains separate)	— ¾ cup
Corn (cooked)	— ½ cup
Onion (chopped)	— 1
Onions (sliced thinly)	— 2
French beans (chopped & boiled)	— ½ cup
Carrots (chopped & boiled)	— ½ cup
Cashewnuts (fried)	— 1 tbsp
Cloves	— 2
Cinnamon (broken into bits)	— 1"
Bay leaves	— 2
Ghee	— as per need
Coriander leaves (chopped)	— 1 tbps
Salt	— to tast

To be ground to a fine paste :

Onion (chopped)	— 1 (small)
Garlic	— 2 cloves

Chilli powder	— 1 tsp
Turmeric powder	— 1 tsp
Coriander seeds	— ½ tsp
Peppercorns	— 2
Cardamoms (peeled)	— 2

Method :

1. Deep fry the sliced onions in hot ghee until golden brown.
2. Heat 2 tbsps ghee in a pan & fry the chopped onion gently.
3. Add the full garam masala & continue frying for sometime.
4. Add the ground masala paste & after frying for some more time add the rice, corn, vegetables, half of the fried onions & salt. Mix thoroughly & cook for a few mts.
5. Serve hot garnished with coriander leaves, fried onions & cashewnuts.

5. JACKFRUIT PULAO

(Serves 4-5)

Ingredients :

Long grain rice (soaked in 2 cups water for 15 mts)	—	250 gms
Raw jackfruit (peeled & cut into small pieces)	—	250 gms
Onions (chopped)	—	2
Ginger	—	½"
Garlic	—	6 cloves
Onions (sliced)	—	2
Red chillies (broken into bits)	—	2-3
Cumin seeds	—	½ tsp
Poppy seeds	—	1 tsp
Coriander seeds	—	2 tsps
Garam masala powder	—	1 tsp
Cloves	—	4
Cinnamon	—	1"

Cardamoms	—	7-8	Peppercorns	—	7-8
Bay leaves	—	3-4	Oil	—	½ cup
Curds	—	½ cup	Salt	—	to taste

Method :

1. Mix together the curds, ground spices & chopped onions.
2. Heat 3 tbsps oil in a pan & fry the jackfruit pieces on a low flame till brown.
3. Add the curd mixture, remove from flame & keep aside.
4. Heat the remaining oil & fry the sliced onion, cinnamon, cardamoms, cloves, peppercorns & bay leaves till light brown.
5. Add he jackfruit mixture & fry till the mixture dries up. Add rice & fry for 3-4 mts.
6. Add salt along with the water in which the rice was soaked & cook till the rice is done. Serve hot.

6. LENTIL PULAO

(Serves 4-5)

Ingredients :

Wheat (boiled)	— handful
Barley (boiled)	— handful
Green gram (boiled)	— handful
Lentil (boiled)	— handful
Gram (boiled)	— handful
Yellow lentil (boiled)	— handful
Long grain rice (washed)	— 250 gms
Onions (chopped finely)	— 3
Tomatoes (chopped finely)	— 4
Oil	— ½ cup
Salt	— to taste

To be ground to a fine paste :

Red chillies (broken into bits)	—	4-5
Mint leaves	—	handful
Coconut (grated)	—	1 tbsp
Cloves	—	6
Cumin seeds	—	1 tsp
Coriander seeds	—	2 tsps
Turmeric powder	—	½ tsp

Method :

1. Heat oil in a large heavy-bottomed pan & fry the onions till golden.
2. Add the ground masala & fry for 5-6 mts more.
3. Add tomatoes & after cooking for 8-10 mts, add the rice along with enough water for the rice to cook.
4. When the rice is done, add the boiled ings, mix very well & serve hot or warm with fresh curds.

7. NAWABI PULAO

(Serves 4-5)

Ingredients :

Long grain rice (boiled with grains separate)	— 1 cup
Onions (chopped)	— 3
Tomatoes (blanched & chopped)	— 2
French beans	— ¼ cup
Carrots	— ¼ cup
Cauliflower (broken into flowerettes)	— ½ cup
Green peas (shelled)	— ½ cup
Green chillies (minced)	— 2-3
Coriander leaves (chopped)	— 1 tbsp
Mint leaves (chopped)	— 1 tbsp
Cashewnuts (chopped)	— 2 tbsps
Raisins	— 2 tbsps

Curry leaves	—	few
Cardamoms	—	2
Cloves	—	2
Ghee	—	5-6 tbsps
Chilli powder	—	1 tsp
Turmeric powder	—	½ tsp
Garam masala powder	—	½ tsp
Mango powder	—	½ tsp
Pepper	—	½ tsp
Salt	—	to taste

Method :

1. Heat ghee in a pan & fry the onions.
2. Add full garam masala, chillies, cashewnuts, curry leaves & fry.
3. Add tomatoes & peas & cook for 2-3 mts.
4. Add the rest of the vegetable & fry, stirring continuously until nearly done.
5. Add coriander leaves, mint leaves, salt & seasoning. Blend well.
6. Add the rice, mix well & place the covered vessel on a hot tawa over a low flame.
7. Cook for 1-2 mts more, stirring continuously.
8. Serve hot garnished with raisins.

8. ONION PULAO

(Serves 2-3)

Ingredients :

Long - grain rice	— 1 cup
Onions (sliced)	— 4
Cardamom	— 1
Cloves	— 2
Ghee	— 6 tbsps
Water	— 2 cups
Chilli powder	— 1 tsp
Turmeric powder	— ½ tsp
Garam masala powder	— ½ tsp
Coriander powder	— 3 tsps
Mango powder	— ½ tsp
Cashewnuts (fried)	— 2 tbsps
Salt	— to taste

Method :

1. Heat the ghee & fry the onions, cardamom & cloves in it lightly.
2. Add seasoning & rice & fry for 5-7 mts more.
3. Add water & salt & cook on a low flame until done.
4. Serve hot garnished with fried cashewnuts.

9. CARROT PULAO

(Serves 2-3)

Ingredients :

Rice (boiled with grains separate)	— 1 cup
Carrots (grated water squeezed out)	— 4
Spring onions (chopped)	— 4
Cardamom	— 1
Cloves	— 2
Cumin seeds (roasted & powdered)	— ½ tsp
Coriander powder	— 3 tsps
Chilli powder	— 1 tsp
Garam masala powder	— ½ tsp
Mango powder	— 1 tsp
Ghee	— 6 tbsps
Water	— 2 cups
Salt	— to taste

Method :

1. Heat the ghee in a pan & fry the cardamom, cloves & onions till transparent.
2. Add the seasoning, carrots & salt.
3. Fry for 1-2 mts so that the colour of carrots is visible.
4. Stir in the rice blend well. Serve hot.

10. PAKORA PULAO

(Serves 2-4)

Ingredients :

Rice (washed & soaked in water for ½ hr)	— 1 cup
Green gram dal (soaked in water for 8 hrs)	— ½ cup
Cinnamon (broken into small pieces)	— 3 cm
Cloves	— 3-4
Cumin seeds	— 1 tbsp
Coriander seeds	— 1 tbsp
Garam masala powder	— ¼ tsp
Red chilli powder	— ½ tbsp
Turmeric powder	— ¼ tsp
Oil	— as per need
Salt	— to taste

Method :

1. Grind the dal to a very fine paste. Immediately fry the pakoras without adding salt or any other ing.
2. Heat oil in a heavy - bottomed pan. Add the cinnamon bits, cloves, cumin seeds, corriander seeds & the rice.
3. Add remaining ings (except the garam masala powder). Add fried pakoras & enough warm water to cook the pulao.
4. A little excess water is needed to cook this pulao because the pakoras absorb some water.
5. Add salt lastly & cook covered on a low flame, putting some water on the lid of the pan.
6. When done, sprinkle the garam masala powder & stir carefully without breaking the pakoras. Serve hot.

11. NAVRATAN PULAO

(Serves 6-8)

Ingredients :

Rice (cooked with grains separate & cooled)	—	2 cups
Onions (sliced thinly)	—	2
Paneer (cubed)	—	2 tbsps
Green peas (shelled & boiled)	—	1 cup
Carrots (boiled & diced)	—	½ cup
Any. stewed fruit (chopped)	—	1 tbsp
Cashewnuts (fried in ghee)	—	1 tbsp
Raisins (fried in ghee)	—	1 tbsp
Shahjeera	—	1 tsp
Cinnamon	—	2"
Cloves	—	2
Cardamoms	—	3
Saffron (soaked in 1 tbsp warm water)	—	¼ tsp
Salt	—	to taste
Onion (sliced)	—	1
Ghee	—	as per need

To be ground to a paste :

Green chillies (chopped)	— 4
Ginger (chopped)	— 1"
Garlic (peeled)	— 4 cloves

Method :

1. Heat ghee in a pan & fry the shahjeera, cinnamon, cloves & cardamons.
2. Add the vegetables, fruit pieces, masala paste, salt & mix well.
3. Add the saffron mixture & mix once again.
4. Serve hot garnished with fried nuts, raisins, fried onions & onion slices.

12. FENUGREEK LEAVES PULAO

(Serves 3-4)

Ingredients :

Rice (boiled with grains separate)	— 250 gms
Fenugreek leaves (chopped)	— 2 bunches
Tamarind juice	— 4 tbsps
Urad dal	— 1 tsp
Chana dal	— 1 tsp
Turmeric powder	— ½ tsp
Jaggery	— to taste
Salt	— to taste
Oil	— 4 tbsps

To be fried in oil separately & ground to a fine paste :

Dry coconut (grated)	— ½ cup
Sesame seeds	— 1 tsp
Red chillies	— 4-5
Cumin seeds	— 1 tsp
Coriander seeds	— 1 tbsp
Asafoetida powder	— pinchful

Method :

1. Dissolve the jaggery in tamarind juice.
2. Heat oil in a large heavy bottomed pan & add the fenugreek leaves, ground paste, turmeric, salt & cook covered until the fenugreek leaves are cooked, without adding water.
3. Add the tamarind mixture & rice.
4. Mix thoroughly & cook on a low flame till the rice turns dry.
5. Serve piping hot.

13. GREEN PEAS PULAO

(Serves 3-4)

Ingredients :

Long grain rice (washed & soaked in water)	— 2 cups
Green peas (shelled)	— 1 cup
Onions (sliced thinly)	— 2
Bay leaves	— 4
Cardamoms	— 4
Cinnamon	— 1"
Cumin seeds	— 1 tsp
Oil	— ½ cup
Cloves	— 5-6
Salt	— to taste

Method :

1. Fry the onions in hot oil till golden crisp. Keep aside 1 tbsp of the fried onions.
2. To the remaining onions, add the peas, all spices & fry for about 2-3 mts.
3. Add 1 cup of water & cook covered on a low flame for 15-20 mts.
4. Then add the rice & enough water for it to cook.
5. Serve hot sprinkled with 1 tbsp of the fried onions.

14. ALOO PULAO

(Serves 3-4)

Ingredients :

Rice (washed & soaked in water for 1 hour)	— 125 gms		
Moong dal (washed & soaked in water for 1 hour)	— 125 gms		
Potatoes (boiled, peeled & fried lightly in oil)	— 1 kg		
Coconuts (grated)	— 2 tbsps		
Spring onions (minced)	— 2		
Curry leaves	— few		
Coriander leaves (chopped)	— 1 tbsp		
Asafoetida powder	— pinchful		
turmeric powder	— ½ tsp		
Chana dal	— 1 tbsp+1 tsp		
Urad dal	— 1 tsp		
Thick tamarind pulp	— 4 tbsps		
Cloves	— 4-5	Cinnamon	— ½"
Cashewnuts (fried)	— 1 tbsp	Salt	— to taste
Red chillies	— 4-5	Oil	— as per need

Method :

1. Fry the red chillies, asafoetida, coconut cloves, 1 tbsp chana dal & cinnamon in oil separately & then grind to a fine paste together.
2. Heat 2 tbsps of oil in large pan & put the urad & chana dals in it.When the dals turn red, add onions, rice & moong dal.
3. Mix very well & pour in enough water so as to cook the rice & dal, till tender & dry.
4. Then add all the remaining ings except coriander leaves & cashewnuts & cook till the rice is tender & well cooked.
5. Serve hot garnished with coriander leaves & cashewnuts.

15. NARIAL KOFTA PULAO

(Serves 6-8)

Ingredients :

For the Pulao :

Long grain rice (washed)				—	1 kg
Coconuts (grated & soaked in 8 cups water)				—	2
Ginger - garlic paste				—	4 tsps
Garam masala powder				—	1 tsp
Cinnamon	—	2"	Cardamoms	—	12
Cumin seeds	—	1 tsp	Cloves	—	20
Oil	—	½ cup	Salt	—	to taste

For the koftas :

Coconuts (grated)				—	2
Coriander leaves (chopped)				—	1 bunch
Mint leaves (chopped)				—	2 tbsps
Onions (chopped)				—	2
Ginger (chopped)	—	1"	Gram flour	—	10 tbsps
Chilli powder	—	1½ tsps	Turmeric powder	—	2 tsps
Oil	—	1 cup	Salt	—	to taste

Method :

1. Blend the coconuts in a liquidiser & extract the coconut milk. Heat oil in a pan & fry the ginger-garlic paste till light brown.Add the rice & fry for 4-5 mts stirring often.
2. Add the coconut milk, garam masala powder, salt & let the rice cook till done. A little water can be added if needed.
3. To prepare the koftas, grind together all ings (except oil) without adding water & mix with the gram flour.
4. Mix well, form into small round balls & fry in hot oil till brown.
5. In serving dish, place half the rice, then, place half the koftas over the rice, put the remaining rice over the koftas & the other half koftas over the rice. Serve hot.

16. EGG PULAO

(Serves 6-8)

Ingredients :

Eggs (hard - boiled & sliced)			— 12
Long grain rice			— 500 gms
Green peas (shelled & boiled in salted water)			— 250 gms
Green chillies (chopped)			— 6
Onions (sliced thinly)			— 3
Cinnamon	— 1"	Cloves	— 4
Chilli powder	— 1½ tbsps	Turmeric powder	— ½ tbsp
Ghee	— 250 gms	Ghee (melted)	— 3 tbsps
Coriander leaves (chopped)			— 1 tbsp
Salt			to taste

To be roasted (without oil) & ground to a paste :

Peppercorns	— 12	Cloves	— 4
Cinnamon	— 1"	Poppy seeds	— 1 tbsp
Cumin seeds	— 1 tsp	Coriander seeds	— 2 tsps

To be ground to a fine paste :

Garlic (peeled) — 8 cloves; Onions (chopped) — 2;
Coconut (grated)—1; Tamarind — lemon-sized ball

Method :

1. Heat ghee in a heavy-bottomed pan & fry the 2 onions, 4 cloves 1 inch cinnamon for 1-2 mts.
2. Add the rice along with enough water & salt & cook the rice till done. Heat melted ghee in a pan & stir fry the sliced onion (1) and green chillies for about 1 mt.
3. Add chilli powder, turmeric, cooked green peas, ground masala pastes, sliced eggs, salt & just enough water to make a thick gravy.
4. Bring to boil, add the coriander leaves & remove from flame. Pour the egg curry onto the hot ghee rice.
5. Mix thoroughly, steam for 2-3 mts on a low flame & serve at once.

17. TASTY MUTTON PULAO (TYPE 1)

(Serves 4-5)

Ingredients :

Mutton (cubed & cooked)	— 250 gms
Long - grain rice (soaked in water for 30 mts)	— 250 gms
Onions	— 2 (large)
Tomatoes—	2 (large)
Ginger - garlic paste	— 2 tsps
Mutton stock	— 2 cups
Cloves	— 8
Cinnamon (broken into bits)	— 1½"
Pure ghee	— 2 tbsps
Sugar	— to taste
Salt	— to taste

Method :

1. In a heavy- bottomed pan, heat the ghee, add the sugar & keep stirring continuously until the sugar melts completely.
2. Add the onions, cloves, cinnamon & fry till brown. Add the ginger - garlic paste & the rice.
3. Fry for about 10-12 mts & add the tomatoes. Continue frying for another 5 mts & add salt along with the stock & a little water if necessary.
4. Stir well & cook covered till almost done. Add the mutton cubes, stir very well & cook for another 5-7 mts. Serve hot.

18. TASTY MUTTON PULAO (TYPE 2)

(Serves 4-6)

Ingredients :

Long grain rice (washed)	—	500 gms
Mutton (washed & chopped)	—	500 gms
Onions (chopped)	—	2
Ginger - garlic paste	—	1 tsp
Mint leaves (chopped)	—	1 tbsp
Coriander leaves (chopped)	—	1 tbsp
Green chillies (chopped)	—	4-5
Curds	—	3 tbsps
Saffron essence	—	¼ tsp
Pulao masala	—	1 tsp
Oil	—	8 tbsps
Eggs (hard - boiled & sliced)	—	2
Salt	—	to taste

Method :

1. Heat half the quantity of oil in a pan & fry the onions till golden.
2. Then add the ginger - garlic paste & fry for a mt. Add the mutton pieces & fry on a low flame, stirring often, for about 8-10 mts.
3. Add 2 cups of water along with salt & pressure cook for 10-12 mts.
4. Mix all ings with the rice with enough water to cook the rice & cook on a low flame for 10-12 mts.
5. When done add essence & serve hot garnished with sliced boiled eggs.

19. CHICKEN PULAO

(Serves 4-6)

Ingredients :

Long grain rice	—	750 gms
Chicken (cleaned & cut into medium pieces)	—	500 gms
Onions (sliced)	—	4
Green chillies (sliced)	—	8
Cloves	—	8
Cinnamon	—	1"
Chilli powder	—	1 tsp
Turmeric powder	—	½ tsp
Ginger (minced)	—	1"
Garlic (minced)	—	8 cloves
Ghee	—	300 gms
Coriander leaves (chopped)	—	1 tbsp
Salt	—	to taste

To be roasted (without oil) & ground to a fine paste :

Peppercorns	— 16
Cloves	— 8
Cinnamon	— 1"
Poppy seeds	— 1 tbsp
Cumin seeds	— 2 tsps
Coriander seeds	— 3 tsps

To be ground to a fine paste :

Onions (chopped)	— 4
Garlic (peeled)	— 8 cloves
Tamarind	— lemon - sized ball
Coconut (grated)	— 1

Method :

1. Heat the ghee in a heavy-bottomed large pan & stir fry the onion (4) & green chillies for 1-2 mts.
2. Then add minced ginger, garlic 8 cloves & 1 inch cinnamon & fry for another 1-2 mts.
3. Add chilli powder, turmeric, chicken pieces, salt & ½ cup water along with the ground masala pastes & cook the chicken partially.
4. Then add the rice & stir for 2-3 mts. Add enough water to cook the rice, salt & cook till the rice is well done.
5. Serve hot garnished with coriander leaves.

20. GREEN MASALA PULAO

(Serves 5-6)

Ingredients :

Long-grain rice (cooked)	— 500 gms
Meat (cubed & boiled)	— 750 gms
Green peas (shelled & boilled)	— 1 cup
Onion (grated)	— 1 (big)
Lemon juice	— 1 tbsp
Bay leaves	— 3-4
Oil	— 3 tbsps
Stock	— 1 cup
Salt	— to taste

To be ground to a fine paste :

Green chillies	— 6-8
Ginger	— 1"
Garlic	— 8 cloves
Coriander leaves	— 1–1½ tbsp
Dry coconut (grated)	— ¼
Cumin seeds	— 1 tsp
Aniseeds	— 1 tsp
Poppy seeds	— 1 tbsp

Method :

1. Heat the oil in a pan & fry the onions with bay leaves till pinkish in colour.
2. Add the ground masala paste & fry until the ghee floats on top.
3. Stir in the peas, meat, salt, stock & lemon juice.
4. Mix well & cook till the mixture thickens.
5. Arrange the rice on top of the mixture & cook (placing the pan on a tawa) covered for 10-12 mts.
6. Serve hot.

21. ARABIAN PULAO
(Serves 3-4)

Ingredients :

Mutton or chicken	— 250 gms
Onions (chopped)	— 2 (small)
Rice (parboiled)	— 1 cup
Ginger - garlic - green chilli paste	— ½ tbs
Tomato sauce	— 1 tbsp
Coconut milk	— ¾ cup
Green peas (shelled & boiled)	— 125 gms
French beans (chopped & boiled)	— 125 gms
Cashewnuts	— 1 tbsp
Sesame seeds (powdered)	— 1 tbsp
Poppy seeds (powdered)	— 1 tbsp
Coriander seeds (powdered)	— ½ tbsp
Cumin seeds (powdered)	— ½ tbsp
Kashmiri chillies (powdered)	— 10
Garam masala powder	— ¼ tbsp
Salt	— to taste
Oil	— 1 tbsp

Method :

1. Add the boiled vegetables, ¼ cup coconut milk & salt to the parboiled rice & cook till the rice is done.
2. Add the ginger - garlic - chilli paste to the mutton or chicken & saute well.
3. Also fry the onions in oil till golden brown. Let cool & when crisp, powder them.
4. Heat oil in a pan & saute all the powdered ings for about 4-5 mts. Add the crushed onions, mutton sauce, leftover coconut milk & about ¾ cup water & let boil on a low flame, till the gravy thickens & oil separates.
5. While serving, put rice on a serving dish, spread the cooked mutton, or chicken over it, garnish with cashewnuts & serve hot.

22. PRAWN PULAO

(Serves 4-5)

Ingredients :

Long - grain rice (boiled in salted water & drained)	— 500 gms
Prawns (cleaned & deveined)	— 750 gm
Lemon juice	— 2 tbsps
Turmeric powder	— ½ tsp
Oil	— ¾ cup
Salt	— to taste

To be ground to a fine paste :

Coconut (grated)	— 1
Green chillies	— 12
Coriander leaves	— 2 tbsps
Garlic	— 25 cloves
Cumin seeds	— 3 tsps

Method :

1. Heat oil in a pan & fry the ground masala paste on a low flame for 15-20 mts.
2. Add turmeric powder, salt, prawns, 1½ cups water & cook till the prawns are tender & the gravy thickens.
3. Mix lemon juice with rice.
4. In a serving dish, put in half the rice, then the prawn mixture & cover with the remaining rice & steam for 15-20 mts.
5. Serve hot.

23. FISH PULAO

(Serves 3-4)

Ingredients :

Long grain rice (soaked in water)	— 1½ cups
Fish - pomfret (cleaned & sliced)	— ½ kg
Onion (sliced thinly)	— 1
Onion seeds	— ½ tsp
Cumin seeds	— 1 tsp
Turmeric powder	— ½ tsp
Oil	— 5 tbsps
Salt	— to taste

Method :

1. Boil the fish with all ings (except onion) in sufficient water till tender.Drain & reserve the stock.
2. Brown the onion in hot oil, add rice, and salt. Fry, stirring continuously till the rice begins to a stick to the pan.
3. Add the reserved stock (water in which the fish was boiled) & cook the rice till tender.
4. Lay the fish on top & cook till the fish begins to break.
5. Serve hot.

24. CRAB PULAO

(Serves 3-4)

Ingredients :

Rice	— 1 cup		
Crabs (washed, boiled, shelled & meat removed)	— 2		
Onions	— 1-2		
Green chillies	— 1-2		
Ginger - garlic (minced)	— 1 tbsp		
Coriander leaves	— 1 tbsp		
Cardamoms	— 2		
Cloves	— 2		
Cinnamon	— ½"		
Shahjeera	— ¼ tsp		
Bay leaf	— 2-3		
Bread crumbs	— $^1/_8$ cup		
Cheese (grated)	— 2 tbsp	Ghee	— as needed
Tomato ketchup	— 1 tbsp	Salt	— to taste
Pepper	— to taste		
Peppercorns	— 2-3		

Method :

1. Grind the green chillies & coriander leaves to a fine paste. Heat little ghee in a pan & fry the onion.
2. Add to it the ground paste along with minced ginger - garlic & fry for a while. Then add the crab meat, salt, pepper & fry.
3. Remove from flame, add the ketchup & cheese powder. Mix well. Tie together the full garam masala in a muslin cloth & put the tightly tied cloth in 2 cups of boiling water.
4. Add the washed rice & cook till the rice is done. Remove the cloth. Add some ghee on top of the rice.
5. In case you have reserved the crab shells, fill them with the prepared rice & chose with bread crumbs. Keep the shells in the leftover rice & bake in a moderately hot oven for about 8-10 mts. Serve hot.

25. INDONESIAN PULAO

(Serves 4-6)

Ingredients :

Long grain rice (washed)	— 2 cups
Chicken (jointed & washed)	— 1
Onions (chopped)	— 2
Bay leaf	— 1
Parsley	— 2 sprigs
Prawns (boiled)	— 1 cup
Crab meat (sliced)	— 1 cup
Coriander- cumin powder	— 1 tbsp
Garam masala powder	— 1 tbsp
Chilli powder	— to taste
Turmeric powder	— ½ tsp
Water	— 6 cups
Salt	— to taste
Oil	— 4 tbsps

Method :

1. Heat the oil in a pan, add the chicken with 6 cups water.
2. Add the onion, bay leaf, parsley, salt, spices & cook till the chicken is tender.
3. Strain the stock, it should be about 4 cups (if less add water to make it 4 cups).
4. Remove bones & shred the chicken. Combine the stock & rice & cook till the rice is tender & dry.
5. Mix in the rest of the ings & serve hot.

26. KASHMIRI PULAO

(Serves 8)

Ingredients :

Long grain rice (soaked in water of 30 mts)	—	2 $^1/_3$ cups
Butter or ghee	—	$^1/_3$ cup
Cumin seeds	—	1 tsp
Cardamoms	—	5
Cinnamon	—	½"
Bay leaves	—	5
Cloves	—	8
Vegetable stock	—	5 cups
Almonds (slivered)	—	¼ cup
Walnuts (shelled & halved)	—	¼ cup
Onion (sliced & fried till crisp)	—	1

Method :

1. Heat the butter or ghee in a large pan & saute the cardamoms, cinnamon, bay leaves, cloves & cumin seeds until brown.
2. Add the drained rice & cook till the grains are transparent stirring continuously to prevent it sticking to the pan.
3. Add the stock with salt to taste & bring to a boil.
4. Cover & simmer until the rice is cooked & the liquid is absorbed.
5. Garnish with almonds, walnuts & onion rings before serving.

27. SWEET RICE PULAO

(Serves 6-8)

Ingredients :

Rice (boiled with grains separate)	— 2 cups
Sugar	— ¾ cup
Dates (chopped)	— 1 tbsp
Glaced cherries (chopped)	— 1 tbsp
Walnuts (chopped after shelling)	— 1 tbsp
Almonds (chopped)	— 1 tbsp
Raisins	— 1 tbsp
Pineapple (chopped)	— 1 tbsp
Apricots (chopped)	— 1 tbsp
Rose essence	— few drops
Yellow Food colouring	— few drops
Rose petals	— few
Fresh cream (whipped)	— 4 tbsps

Method :

1. Add sugar, cream, colour & essence to the rice.
2. Arrange the rice, fruits & nuts in a layer in bowl.
3. Start & finish with a layer of rice.
4. Decorate with petals of rose. Press down very firmly & cover with aluminium foil.
5. Place the bowl in a steamer & steamer for half on hour. Unmould & serve hot.

28. TOMATO & CAPSICUM PULAO

(Serves 5-6)

Ingredients :

Long-grain rice (washed & drained thoroughly)	—	500 gms
Onions (chopped)	—	2 (medium)
Tomatoes (pureed)	—	5 (big)
Capsicums (slitted on top & seeds removed)	—	5 (big)
Coriander leaves (chopped)	—	1 tbsp
Ginger-garlic paste	—	½ tsp
Cinnamon (broken into pieces)	—	2"
Cloves	—	4-5
Cardamoms	—	3-4
Asafoetida powder	—	pinchful
Cumin seeds	—	1 tsp
Turmeric powder	—	½ tsp
Cheese (grated)	—	½ cup
Salt	—	to taste

Method :

1. Heat ¼ cup oil in a large heavy-bottomed pan & fry the onions in it till light brown. Add the whole garam masala & fry a while. Add asafoetida powder & cumin seeds & fry for a minute.
2. Lastly, add the rice, salt & enough water to cook it. Cook till done. Heat 3 tbsp oil in a pan & fry the ginger-garlic.
3. Add tomato puree, turmeric & salt. Cook covered for about 10 mts over a low flame. Keep aside.
4. Stuff the capsicums with the prepared rice. Heat the remaining oil in a pan & put in the stuffed capsicums very carefully.
5. Fry covered for about 10 mts till the capsicums soften. Remove & arrange in a serving dish. Also arrange the left-over rice around the capsicums. Pour tomato gravy over & serve hot garnished with coriander leaves & cheese.

29. EGG PULAO WITH YAM

(Serves 3-4)

Ingredients :

Rice (washed & drained thoroughly)	— 1½ cups
Yam (peeled, cubed & boiled till tender)	— 250 gms
Eggs (hard-boiled, peeled & deep fried in ghee till brown)	— 6
Onion (sliced thinly)	— 1 (big)
Whole garam masala	— 1 tsp
Bay leaves	— 2
Caraway seeds	— ½ tsp
Curds (beaten with ½ tsp sugar)	— 1 cup
Saffron (powdered)	— ¼ tsp
Ghee	— 3 tbsp
Salt	— to taste

To be ground to a fine paste :

Green chillies	— 6-8
Ginger	— ½"
Garlic	— 6-8 cloves

Method :

1. Heat the ghee in a pan & fry the onions till golden.
2. Add the whole garam masala, bay leaves, ground masala paste, caraway seeds & fry for 2-3 mts.
3. Add the curds & yam.
4. Cook over a very low flame for 10-12 mts till the mixture thickens.
5. Then add the rice & 2½ cups water & cook till all water is absorbed.
6. Stir in the eggs & cook covered after placing the pan on a tawa for 15-20 mts. Serve hot.

C. RECIPES FOR BIRYANI

1. VEGETABLE BIRYANI

(Serves 7-8)

Ingredients :

Long grain rice (boiled with grains separate)	— 500 gms
Mixed vegetables of your choice (chopped & boiled)	— 500 gms
Onions (sliced thinly)	— 4
Cashewnuts (fried)	— 1 tbsp
Salt	— to taste
Ghee	— 250 gms

To be ground to a fine paste :

Coconut (grated)	— 1
Mint leaves	— 1 bunch
Green chillies	— 8
Aniseeds	— 1 tsp

Method :

1. Heat the ghee in a large heavy-bottomed pan, add the ground masala paste, cooked vegetables, fried onions & cashewnuts.
2. Add the cooked rice, mix well & serve hot.

2. SPROUTED MATH BIRYANI WITH PANEER

(Serves 6-8)

Ingredients :

Long - grain rice	— 1 cup
Sprouted math	— 2 cups
Tomato (chopped finely)	— 1
Carrot (chopped finely)	— 1
Potato (chopped finely)	— 1
Paneer (cubed)	— 200 gms
Curds	— 1 cup
Cashewnuts	— 1 tbsp
Raisins	— 1 tbsp
Coriander leaves (chopped)	— 1 tbsp
Ghee	— 4 tbsps
Salt	— to taste
Red chillies (broken into bits)	— 6
Coconut (grated) — 1	Onion — 1
Cumin seeds — 1 tsp	Turmeric powder — ½ tsp

Method :

1. Mix together the coconut, red chillies, cumin seeds, onion & turmeric powder. Add 2 cups water & blend in a liquidiser to extract coconut milk. Strain.
2. Heat 2 tbsps of ghee & fry the raisins & nuts. Keep aside. To the same pan, add the math, carrot, polato & cook covered till almost cooked.
3. Heat the remaining ghee, add the rice & fry for sometime. Add the tomato, coconut milk, salt & cook covered until almost cooked.
4. Add the cooked vegetables, curds & paneer at this stage & cook covered till well done.
5. Serve piping hot garnished with fried nuts, raisins & corriander leaves.

3. MASOOR BIRYANI

(Serves 4)

Ingredients :

Whole masoor (soaked in water for 6 hrs)	— ½ cup
Rice (boiled)	— 1 cup
Onions (sliced thinly)	— 2
Onion (chopped)	— 1
Tomatoes	— 1
Ghee	— as per need
Saffron (dissolved in 1 tsp warm milk)	— few strands
Salt	— to taste

To be ground to a fine paste :

Red chillies	— 4
Garlic	— 2 cloves
Ginger	— ½"
Poppy seeds	— 2 tsps
Coriander seeds	— 1½ tsps
Cumin seeds	— ¾ tsp

Method :

1. Fry the sliced onions in ghee till golden brown in colour.
2. Heat 2 tbsps of ghee in a heavy-bottomed pan & fry the chopped onion lightly. Add the ground paste & fry for few mts.
3. Then add the tomatoes & continue frying for 1-2 mts. Add the masoor along with salt & ½ cup water.
4. To the cooked rice, add the saffron mixture, fried onions, salt & mix very well.
5. In a large baking tray, spread 1 tbsp ghee & make four layers by spreading $^1/_3$ of rice, then ½ of the masoor, next spreading a further $^1/_3$ of the rice & lastly the remaining masoor & rice.
6. Bake covered in a preheated oven at 450°F for 15-20 mts. Serve hot.

4. TRADITIONAL CHICKEN BIRYANI

(Serves 7-9)

Ingredients :

Chicken (cut into pieces)	— 1 (medium)
Onion (chopped)	— 1
Pure ghee	— 2 tbsps
Lemon juice	— 2 tbsps
Oil	— 2 tbsps
For the rice :	
Long - grain rice	— 1 kg
Milk	— 1 tbsp
Peppercorns	— ¼ tsp
Cinnamon (broken into bits)	— 1"
Bay leaves	— 3
Cardamoms	— 4
Yellow food colour	— few drops
Salt	— to taste

To be ground to a fine paste :

Onion (chopped)	— 1
Kashmiri red chillies	— 10
Coriander leaves	— 3 tbsps
Green chillies	— 4-5
Coriander seeds	— 1 tbsp
Peppercorns	— ½ tsp
Ginger	— 1"
Garlic	— 15 cloves
Mint leaves	— few
Mace	— 1 petal

Method :

1. Wash & soak the rice in water for 30 mts. Bring enough water to a boil & add all other ings (except rice). Add rice & cook till half - done. Drain thoroughly & keep aside.
2. Heat oil in a pan (heavy-bottomed) & fry the chopped onion till well browned. Add the ground masala paste & continue frying until the oil separates. Add the chicken & saute till it is well - coated with the masala.
3. Add salt little water & cook covered, until done. Add lemon juice & simmer till the gravy is very thick, but not

dry. In heavy - bottomed big pan, smear a little ghee & spread a layer of the cooked rice. Put the gravy from the cooked chicken over it.

4. Spread another layer of the rice over it. Dissolve the food colour in milk & sprinkle half of it over the rice.
5. Put all the chicken pieces along with the leftover gravy & top it with a layer of rice. Melt the remaining ghee and pour it along with the coloured milk over the rice. Cook covered on a low flame for about 40-45 mts. Serve hot.

5. YUMMY CHICKEN BIRYANI (TYPE 1)

(Serves 4-6)

Ingredients :

Long grain rice (washed)	— 1½ cups
Chicken (cleaned & cut into pieces)	— 1 kg
Onions (sliced)	— 5
Tomatoes (chopped)	— 2
Ginger - garlic paste	— 2 tsps
Curds (beaten)	— 3 tbsps
Cinnamon (broken into bits)	— 2"
Cardamons	— 6
Peppercorns	— 8-10
Bay leaf	— 1-2
Chilli powder	— 1 tsp
Saffron (soaked in ¼ cup warm milk)	— 1 tsp
Cashewnuts (fried)	— 1½ tbsp
Raisins (fried)	— 1½ tbsp
Oil	— ¾ cup
Eggs (hard - boiled & sliced)	— to garnish
Salt	— to taste

Method :

1. Parboil the rice with half the garam masala & keep aside. Heat oil in a pan & fry the onions till crisp & brown cursh half & keep aside.
2. To the same oil, add the remaining spices, ginger - garlic paste & fry for 1-2 mts. Add chicken & stir continuously till it turns golden in colour.
3. Add the curds, tomatoes, crushed onions & half the saffron mixture. Add ½ cup water & cook covered on a low flame for 15-20 mts. Remove from flame.
4. Spread rice over the chicken mixture, add the remaining saffron mixture & cook covered on a low flame for 10-15 mts.
5. Serve hot sprinkled with nuts & raisins & garnished with fried onions & sliced boiled eggs.

6. YUMMY CHICKEN BIRYANI (TYPE 2)

(Serves 5-7)

Ingredients :

Long-grain rice (washed & soaked in water)			— 750 gms
Chicken (jointed & washed well)			— 1 (medium)
Onions (sliced)			— 2
Thick tomato puree			— ½ cup
Curds (beaten)			— ½ cup
Green cardamoms	— 2	Cinnamon	— ½"
Cloves	— 2	Bay leaves	— 2
Oil or ghee	— ½ cup	Salt	— to taste

To be ground to a fine paste :

Onion (chopped)	— 1 (large)	Ginger (chopped)	— 1"
Garlic (peeled)	— 3-4 cloves	Cumin seeds	— 1 tsp
Green chillies (chopped)			— 7-8
Poppy seeds	— ½ tsp	Aniseeds	— ½ tsp
Coriander leaves (chopped)			— 1 tbsp
Cinnamon	— ½"	Cardamoms	— 1-2

Cloves	— 2	Peppercorns	— few
Turmeric powder			— ½ tsp

Method :

1. Cook the rice with onions, cloves, cardamoms & bay leaves till ¾ done. Keep aside.
2. Heat the ghee or oil in a heavy-bottomed large pan & fry the chicken pieces along with all the ground masala paste, till dry & brown.Add tomato puree & curds.
3. Add enough water to cook the chicken & for a thick gravy.
4. Add the rice & stir gently. Cook on a low flame till the rice is cooked & dry.
5. Serve hot garnished with fried onions.

7. MUTTON BIRYANI

(Serves 7-8)

Ingredients :

Boneless mutton (chopped)	— ½ kg
Long grain rice (washed)	— ½ kg
Onion - ginger - garlic paste	— 2 tbsps
Onions (sliced thinly & fried)	— 2 (small)
Green chillies (minced)	— 6
Garam masala powder	— 1 tsp
Green cardamoms	— 3
Cloves — 2-3 Bay leaves	— 2
Curds (beaten) — ½ cup Ghee	— ½ cup
Chilli powder	— to taste
Turmeric powder	— ¼ tsp
Kewra essence	— few drops
Yellow food colour (mixed with water)	— few drops
Salt	— to taste
Cumin seeds	— ½ tsp

Method :

1. Heat the ghee in a pressure cooker, add cumin seeds & fry for 2-3 mts.
2. Add the meat, salt, chilli powder, garam masala powder, onion-ginger-garlic paste, cardamoms, cloves, bay leaves & fry for 1-2 mts.
3. Add the curds & enough water to cook the meat & enough water remains to cook the rice. Pressure cook till the meat is tender.
4. Then add the rice, chillies & essence. Stir gently & cook tightly covered on a low flame till the rice is tender & dry.
5. Sprinkle coloured water over the rice. Serve hot garnished with fried onions.

8. MUGHLAI BIRYANI

(Serves 3-4)

Ingredients :

Long grain rice (boiled with grains separate)	— 1 cup
Onions (sliced)	— 2
Carrots (diced & boiled)	— ¼ cup
French beans (shredded & boiled)	— ¼ cup
Green peas (shelled & boiled)	— ½ cup
Green chillies (minced)	— 2
Ginger	— ½"
Coriander (chopped)	— ½ tbsp
Sour curds (beaten)	— ½ cup
Chilli powder	— ½ tsp
Turmeric Powder	— ½ tsp
Coriander powder	— 2 tsps
Garam masala powder	— ½ tsp
Saffron (mixed with a little water)	— few strands
Raisins	— 3 tbsps
Ghee	— 4 tbsps
Salt	— to taste

Method :

1. Grind together the green chillies, coriander & ginger to a fine paste. Keep aside. **2.** Heat the ghee in a large pan, add garam masala, onions & fry. Add the boiled vegetables, seasoning & fry for another 3-4 mts. Keep aside. **3.** Divide the rice into 3 portions & the vegetables into 2 portions. Tint one portion of the rice green by mixing it with the ground masala paste. **4.** Tint the second portion yellow by adding saffron mixture. Keep the third portion white. Take a large serving dish & place in it a layer of white rice. **5.** Spread a layer of the vegetables mixture over it. Cover the vegetables with the green rice. Then cover the green rice with vegetables & finally spread a layer of saffron rice. Garnish with raisins & serve.

9. AHMEDI MUTTON BIRYANI

(Serves 6-8)

Ingredients :

Rice (washed, parboiled, drained & cooled)			— 500 gms
Mutton (cleaned, cut into large pieces, washed & draind)			— 1 kg
Onions (sliced thinly)			— 4 (big)
Curds (beaten)			— 2 cups
Ginger (ground to a paste)			— 2"
Garlic (ground to a paste)			— 1 pod
Chilli powder			— 2½ tsp
Coriander seeds (powdered)			— 2 tsp
Cinnamon (broken into bits)			— 2 "
Cardamoms			— 6-7
Bay leaves	— 4	Cloves	— 6-8
Peppercorns	— 6-8	Ghee	— 250 gms
Sugar	— 1 tbsp	Salt	— to taste

Method :

1. Heat the ghee in a pan & fry the whole garam masala till brown.
2. Add onions & fry till brown. Add the powdered spices, sugar, salt & fry for another 4-5 mts.
3. Add 2-3 cups of hot water & cook uncovered till the meat is well-cooked. Add curds & cook till the mixture thickens.
4. Take a large pan, lay a layer of ricc (half quantity) & spread half quantity of the mutton mixture over it.
5. Cover with the remaining rice & the meat. Place the pan on a tawa & cook covered for about 20-25 mts. Serve hot with curds or raita.

(D) RECIPES FOR KHICHREE

1. INSTANT KHICHREE

(Serves 2-4)

Ingredients :

Rice			— 1 cup
Split green moong dal			— ½ cup
Onion (chopped)			— 1
Turmeric powder			— ¼ tsp
Green chillies (chopped)			— 2
Coriander leaves (chopped)			— ¼ tsp
Peppercorns	— 3-4	Cloves	— 4
Salt	— to taste	Asafoetida powder	— 2 pinchfuls

For the seasoning :

Pure ghee or vanaspati	— 2 tbsps
Cumin seeds	— 1 tsp

Method :

1. Combine together all the ings for the khichree (except the seasoning ings) & pressure cook upto 4 whistles.
2. Prepare the seasoning by heating the ghee along with cumin seeds & add to the khichree.
3. Mix well & serve hot; along with fresh curds.

2. KHICHREE WITH KADHI

(Serves 3-4)

Ingredients :

For the khichree :

Rice	— 1 cup
Yellow moong dal	— ½ cup
Turmeric powder	— $^1/_8$ tsp
Salt	— to taste

For the kadhi :

Curds	— 125 gms
Gram flour	— ½ cup
Green chilli - garlic paste	— 1 tbsp
Curry leaves (crushed coarsely)	— few
Turmeric powder	— $^1/_8$ tsp
Cloves	— 3-4
Cinnamon	— ½"

Salt	— to taste	Sugar	— to taste
Oil	— 2 tsps	Water	— 2 cup

Method :

1. Prepare the khichree by cooking together the ings for the khichree.
2. Whisk the curds along with gram flour. Add water & the ground paste.
3. Also add the turmeric, salt, sugar & cook on a high flame till the flour is well cooked, stirring continuously.
4. Heat oil & prepare a seasoning with cloves, cinnamon & curry leaves.
5. Serve hot with khichree.

3. YUMMY PRAWN KHICHREE

(Serves 4-6)

Ingredients :

Prawns (shelled)	— 175 gms
Rice	— 225 gms
Green peas (shelled)	— 125 gms
Onions (chopped)	— 2
Tomatoes (chopped)	— 2
Ginger-garlic paste	— 1 tsp
Chilli powder	— 1½ tsps
Turmeric powder	— ¼ tsp
Coriander - cumin powder	— 1 tsp
Bay leaves	— 2
Cardamoms	— 3-4
Ghee	— ¼ cup
Oil	— ¼ cup
Salt	— to taste

Method :

1. Heat the oil in a heavy-bottomed pan & fry the onions till well browned. Add the tomatoes & fry for 8-10 mts more.
2. Add the prawns & fry for few more mts. Then add the peas & cook covered, until done.
3. Heat oil in a large heavy-bottomed pan. Add bay leaves, cardamoms, rice & fry for a few mts.
4. Add salt, enough water & cook till almost done. Spread the prawn mixture on top & cook covered for about 8-10 mts on a low flame.
5. Pour the remaining ghee over it & bake, covered, in a moderately hot even for 30-35 mts. Serve hot.

4. FRIED VEGETABLE KHICHREE

(Serves 4-6)

Ingredients :

Long grain rice (washed soaked in water for 30 mts)	— 1 cup
Yellow moong dal (soaked in water for 30 mts)	— ¼ cup
Split (green gram) moong dal (soaked in water for 30 mts)	— ¼ cup
Green peas (shelled & parboiled)	— ¼ cup
French beans (chopped & parboiled)	— ¼ cup
Carrots (scraped, diced & parboiled)	— ¼ cup
Ghee (melted)	— ½ cup
Water	— 2 ¾ cup
Salt	— to taste

Method :

1. Heat the ghee in a pan & add to it the drained rice & dals.
2. Fry for about 5-7 mts, stirring continuously.
3. Add water & cook covered until almost done.
4. Then add all the vegetables, place on a hot pan & cook on a low flame until well done. Serve hot.

5. BAJRA KHICHREE

(Serves 3-4)

Ingredients :

Rice (washed & drained)	— ½ cup
Bajra (washed, drained & dried)	— 1 cup
Yellow moong dal	— ½ cup
Coconut (desiccated)	— ¼ cup
Garlic (minced)	— 5-6 cloves
Turmeric powder	— ¼ tsp
Chilli powder	— to taste
Coriander leaves (chopped)	— 1 tbsp
Salt	— to taste

Method :

1. Heat 1 tbsp oil in a pan & add to it 3½ cups water.
2. Once the water boils, add the powdered spices, salt & mix well.
3. Let cook till bajra, the rice & dal are tender.
4. Add coriander & coconut once the khichree is cooked. Serve hot.

Note : *Just before serving, heat the remaining oil & fry the garlic for half a mt. Pour this seasoning over the khichree & serve.*

6. SWEET KHICHREE

(Serves 3-4)

Ingredients :

Fine-quality rice (washed, drained, dried, roasted, washed & drained)	— 1 cup
Moong (washed & drained)	— ¾ cup
Fresh coconut (desiccated finely)	— 1 cup
Jaggery	— to taste
Cardamoms (peeled & powdered)	— 4
Pure ghee	— 4 tbsp
Cashewnuts (broken into bits)	— 8-10
Salt	— pinchful